D1611908

Under the Sea
Shrimp

by Deborah Nuzzolo

Consulting Editor: Gail Saunders-Smith, PhD

Consultant: Ray Davis
Senior Vice President, Zoological Operations
Georgia Aquarium

Capstone
press

Mankato, Minnesota

Pebble Plus is published by Capstone Press,
151 Good Counsel Drive, P.O. Box 669, Mankato, Minnesota 56002.
www.capstonepress.com

1 2 3 4 5 6 12 11 10 09 08 07

Library of Congress Cataloging-in-Publication Data
Nuzzolo, Deborah.
    Shrimp / by Deborah Nuzzolo.
    p. cm.—(Pebble plus. Under the sea)
    Summary: "Simple text and photographs describe shrimp, their body parts, and what they do"—Provided
by publisher.
    Includes bibliographical references and index.
    ISBN-13: 978-1-4296-0035-4 (hardcover)
    ISBN-10: 1-4296-0035-7 (hardcover)
    1. Shrimps—Juvenile literature. I. Title. II. Series.
QL444.M33N89 2008
595.3'88—dc22   2006102230

Editorial Credits
Mari Schuh, editor; Juliette Peters, set designer; Kim Brown, book designer; Charlene Deyle and Scott Thoms,
    photo researchers

Photo Credits
Getty Images Inc./Jane Burton, cover
Minden Pictures/Chris Newbert, 20–21
Seapics/Dennis Sabo, 16–17; Mark Conlin, 4–5
Shutterstock/Marianne Bones, 1; Mark Aplet, 10–11; Olga Bogatyrenko, 12–13
Tom Stack & Associates, Inc./Dave Fleetham, 8–9, 14–15, 18–19; Ed Robinson, 6–7

Note to Parents and Teachers

The Under the Sea set supports national science standards related to the diversity
and unity of life. This book describes and illustrates shrimp. The images support early
readers in understanding the text. The repetition of words and phrases helps early
readers learn new words. This book also introduces early readers to subject-specific
vocabulary words, which are defined in the Glossary section. Early readers may need
assistance to read some words and to use the Table of Contents, Glossary, Read More,
Internet Sites, and Index sections of the book.

Table of Contents

What Are Shrimp?. 4
Body Parts. 8
What Shrimp Do 14
Under the Sea. 20

Glossary 22
Read More 23
Internet Sites. 23
Index .24

What Are Shrimp?

Shrimp are skinny sea animals with strong shells.

Some shrimp are
as small as a raisin.
Other shrimp grow
as long as a pencil.

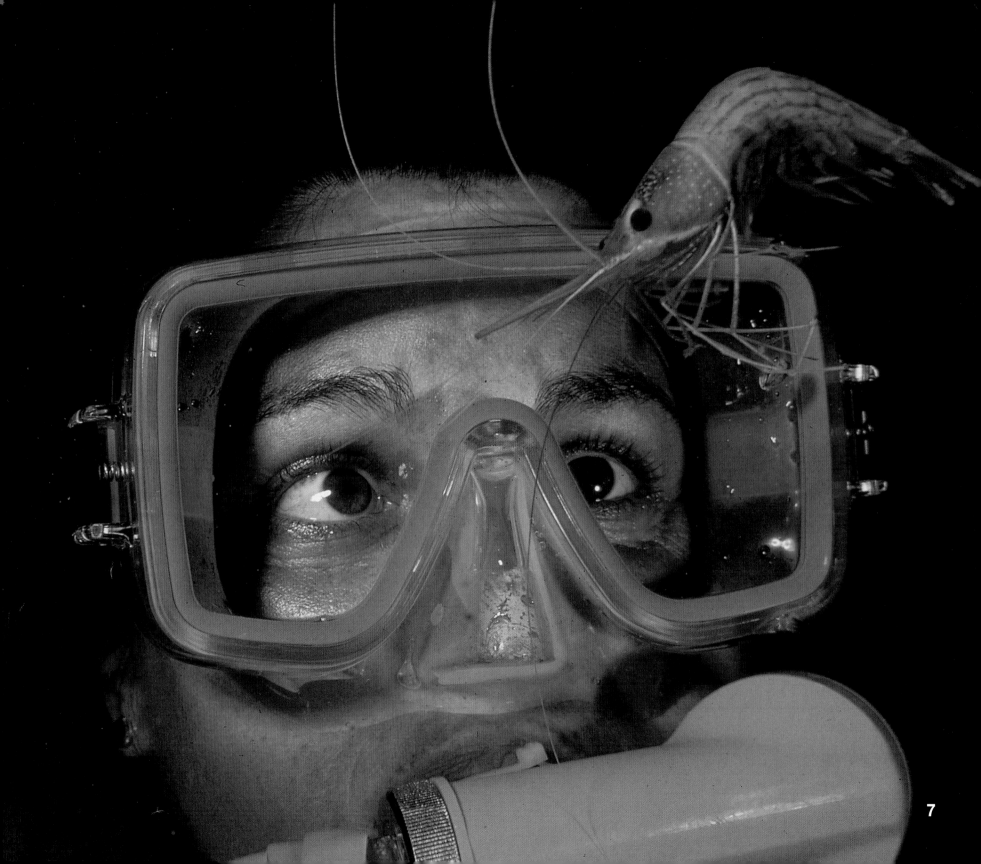

Body Parts

Shrimp have long legs. Some of their legs have pincers to grab food.

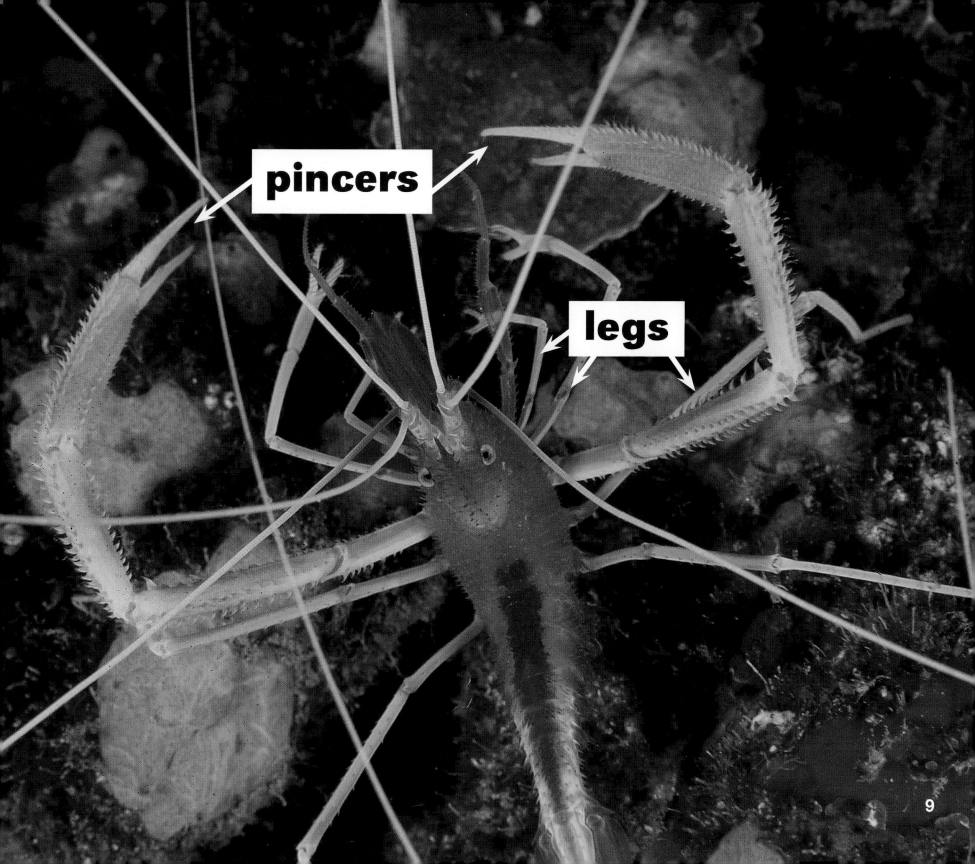

pincers

legs

9

Shrimp use their flat tails
to steer as they swim.

tail

Shrimp wave their antennas
to touch and smell.

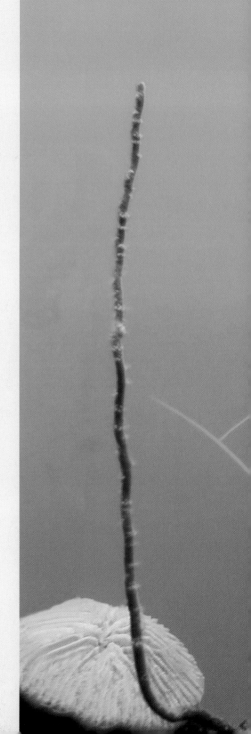

antennas

What Shrimp Do

Shrimp eat
tiny animals and plants.
Cleaner shrimp pick
food off fish.

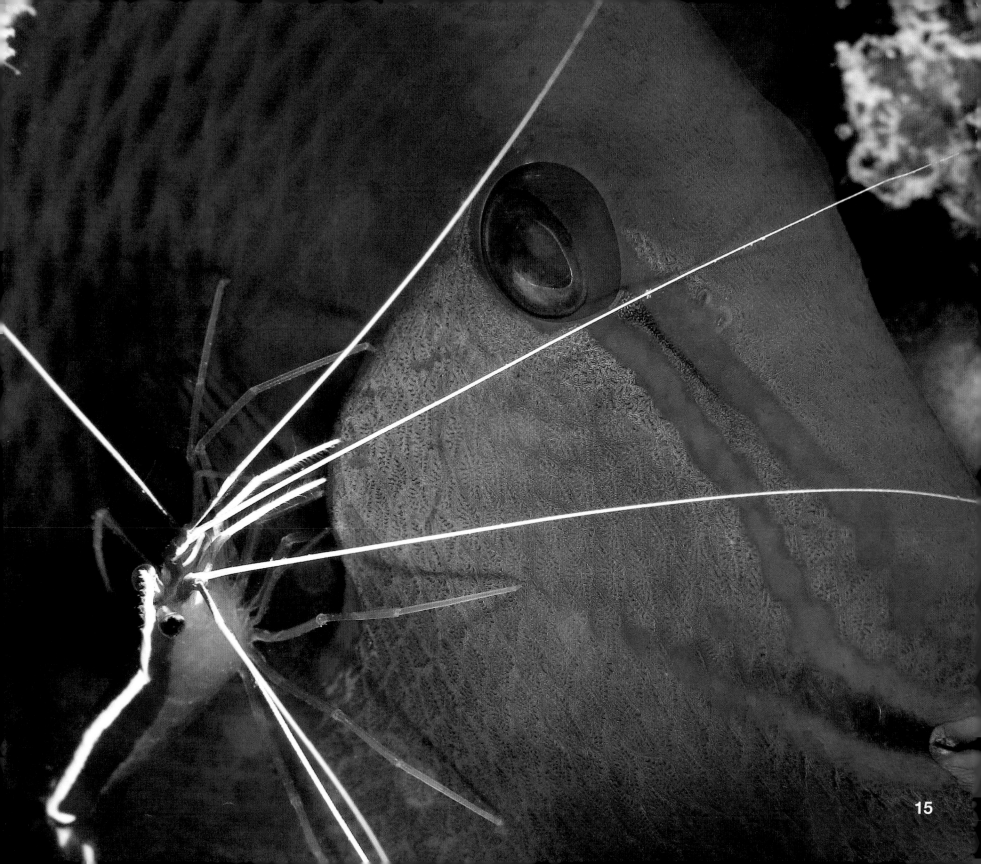

Shrimp paddle forward
with their legs.

Shrimp hide from enemies
in corals, sand, and plants.
Their color helps them
blend in.

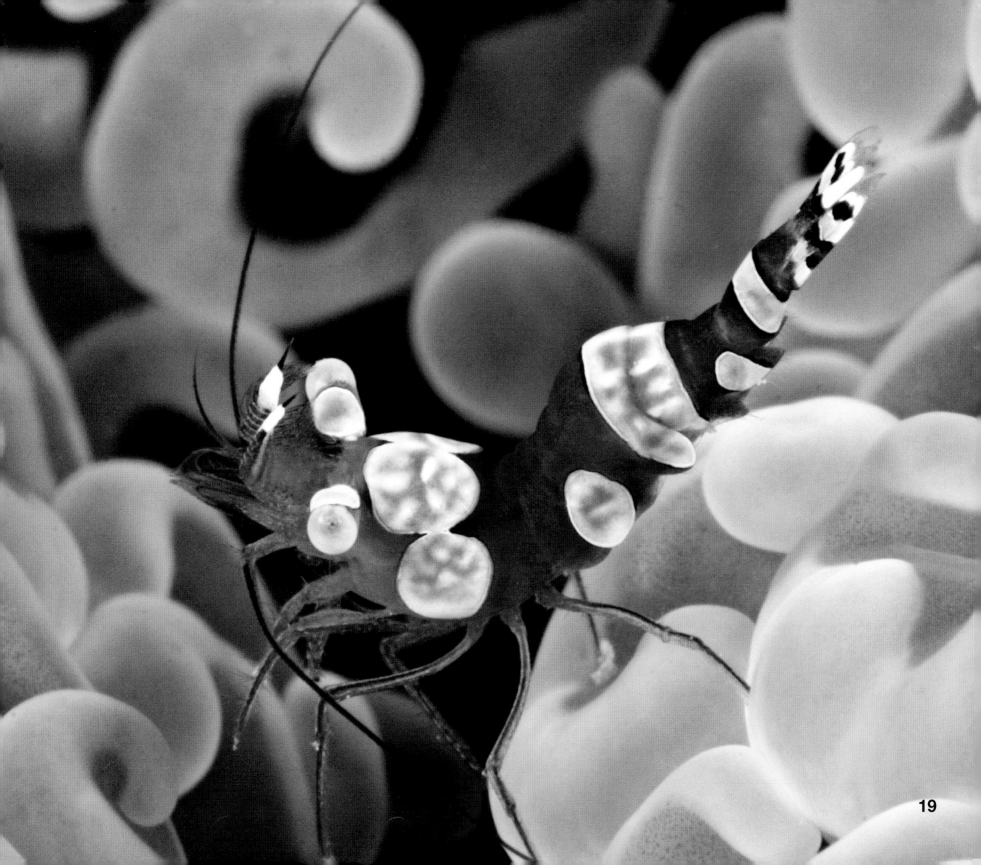

Under the Sea

Shrimp scurry and swim
under the sea.

Glossary

antenna—a feeler on a shrimp's head; shrimp use antennas to touch and smell.

coral—an ocean animal that usually lives in groups; hard coral groups look like colorful rocks.

paddle—to move about in water using the legs, hands, or feet

pincer—a claw used to grab and hold food

scurry—to run with short, quick steps

shell—a hard covering on the outside of some animals

steer—to guide or direct

Read More

Lindeen, Carol. *Life in an Ocean.* Living in a Biome. Mankato, Minn.: Capstone Press, 2004.

Sill, Cathryn P. *About Crustaceans: A Guide for Children.* Atlanta: Peachtree Publishers, 2004.

Stone, Lynn M. *Shrimp.* Science under the Sea. Vero Beach, Fla.: Rourke, 2003.

Internet Sites

FactHound offers a safe, fun way to find Internet sites related to this book. All of the sites on FactHound have been researched by our staff.

Here's how:

1. Visit *www.facthound.com*

2. Choose your grade level.

3. Type in this book ID **1429600357** for age-appropriate sites. You may also browse subjects by clicking on letters, or by clicking on pictures and words.

4. Click on the **Fetch It** button.

FactHound will fetch the best sites for you!

Index

antennas, 12

color, 18

eating, 14

fish, 14

food, 8, 14

hiding, 18

legs, 8, 16

pincers, 8

shells, 4

size, 6

smelling, 12

swimming, 10, 20

tails, 10

touching, 12

Word Count: 95
Grade: 1
Early-Intervention Level: 14